**Cherish**

# *The Night Before Christmas*

Poems, Songs, and Thoughts for Christmas

Publications International, Ltd.

©1998 Priscilla Hillman.
Licensed by Enesco Corporation, owner
of the CHERISHED TEDDIES trademark.

Quotations on pages 9 (bottom), 15 (bottom), 29, and 37 (bottom) written by Priscilla Hillman, artist and creator of the Cherished Teddies™ collection. Other quotations compiled and written by Kelly Womer, a freelance writer whose work has appeared in several national collectibles publications.

Photography by Brian Warling.

Photo styling by Lisa Wright.

Acknowledgments:
Excerpt on p. 13 from *Christmas Joy*, by Susan Branch; Little, Brown and Company, publishers.

Copyright © 1998 Publications International, Ltd. All rights reserved. This book may not be reproduced or quoted in whole or in part by any means whatsoever without written permission from:

Louis Weber, C.E.O.
Publications International, Ltd.
7373 North Cicero Avenue
Lincolnwood, Illinois 60646

Permission is never granted for commercial purposes.

Manufactured in China.

8 7 6 5 4 3 2 1

ISBN: 0-7853-2928-5

## THE NIGHT BEFORE CHRISTMAS

*When you make your Christmas wish list, don't forget to wish for those things that can't be bought: family get-togethers, merry laughter, fond memories, and peace. These gifts are priceless.*

# THE NIGHT BEFORE CHRISTMAS

*He spoke not a word, but went straight to his work, And filled all the stockings; then turned with a jerk, And laying his finger aside his nose, And giving a nod, up the chimney he rose.*

—Clement C. Moore,
*The Night Before Christmas*

# The Night Before Christmas

# THE NIGHT BEFORE CHRISTMAS

## The Night Before Christmas

*If home is where the heart is, then Christmas makes everyone feel right at home.*

*Why do people love teddie bears? Because they don't eat much, never betray a secret, never swear, and never, never steal all the covers.*

— Priscilla Hillman

THE NIGHT BEFORE CHRISTMAS

*When the weather outside is frightful, cuddle up in your cushiest chair with your favorite teddy bear and blanket, sip a homemade cup of hot chocolate, and open a treasured Christmas story. That's what makes the season delightful!*

# THE NIGHT BEFORE CHRISTMAS

# THE NIGHT BEFORE CHRISTMAS

## The Night Before Christmas

*The gift of fun: take time to romp in the snow—make snow angels and snowmen—go ice skating. Come in cold and frosty to something hot from the stove.*

—Susan Branch,
*Christmas Joy*

# The Night Before Christmas

## The Night Before Christmas

*Christmas brings everyone closer together—even when family and friends are many miles away. Christmas bridges any distance, great or small.*

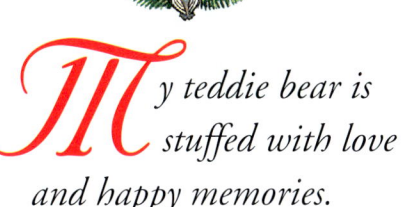

*My teddie bear is stuffed with love and happy memories.*

—Priscilla Hillman

## The Night Before Christmas

*May the peace of Christmas
comfort you.
May the love of Christmas bless you.
May the joy of Christmas
surround you.*

*Christmas does a heart good.
Its blissful blessings and
timeless treasures can only add
happiness to everyone's life.*

# The Night Before Christmas

# THE NIGHT BEFORE CHRISTMAS

# THE NIGHT BEFORE CHRISTMAS

*Make yours a teddie bear Christmas. Teddie bear ornaments to decorate the tree. Teddie bear gingerbread cookies to sweeten the season. Teddie bear wrapping paper to cover all the gifts. Teddie bear dreams to bring warm wishes. And, of course, lots of teddie bears to celebrate with you!*

# The Night Before Christmas

*The chill of winter only makes the kitchen warmer, the fireplace cozier, the company friendlier, and the conversation merrier. Come out of the cold and into the holidays!*

# The Night Before Christmas

# THE NIGHT BEFORE CHRISTMAS

## THE NIGHT BEFORE CHRISTMAS

*In the North Pole, Santa's elves busily make their toys, clicking and clacking, hammering and clamoring, painting and putting the finishing touches on the gifts that will bring a smile to every boy and girl. On Christmas Eve, the elves say farewell to their toys all stacked on the sleigh and wave good-bye as Santa goes on his merry way. For elves, there's never a happier day!*

## THE NIGHT BEFORE CHRISTMAS

*The heart grows fonder at Christmas. It's a welcome home for family, friends, and loved ones whom you may not have seen since the last holiday. It's a welcome sight to see homes all decorated with the season's joy. It's a welcome feeling to know that the spirit that embraces Christmas is the same one that gleams in your heart.*

# THE NIGHT BEFORE CHRISTMAS

# THE NIGHT BEFORE CHRISTMAS

# The Night Before Christmas

*Christmas is a joyous jubilation, a cheerful celebration. It's a festive party for friends, quiet moments for two, or solitary reflections for one. Christmas is whatever you make it to be. Make it special. Make it yours.*

# THE NIGHT BEFORE CHRISTMAS

# The Night Before Christmas

*A teddie bear's real charm is in being huggable.*

—Priscilla Hillman

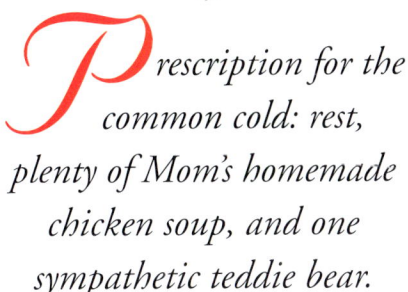

*Prescription for the common cold: rest, plenty of Mom's homemade chicken soup, and one sympathetic teddy bear.*

—Priscilla Hillman

## The Night Before Christmas

*The best Christmas gifts are those that come from your heart because they mean the most to you... and surely they will mean the world to the lucky person who receives the splendid token of your thoughtfulness.*

# The Night Before Christmas

# THE NIGHT BEFORE CHRISTMAS

## THE NIGHT BEFORE CHRISTMAS

*It's a heartwarming, foot-stomping, gift-bearing, memory-making, eye-opening, snow-falling, tree-trimming, happy-greeting, homemade, never-ending Christmas!*

## The Night Before Christmas

*The first snow seems more lovely than all the others that follow. It brings back warm memories of winters past and it welcomes winter present. It blankets the season with nature's beauty.*

# The Night Before Christmas

# THE NIGHT BEFORE CHRISTMAS

# The Night Before Christmas

*If it weren't for Christmas cards, some friends would miss the opportunity to catch up on the year's events and celebrate the year that's yet to come.*

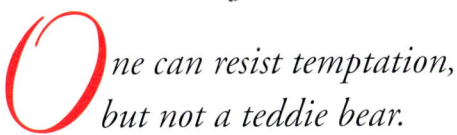

*One can resist temptation, but not a teddie bear.*

— Priscilla Hillman

# THE NIGHT BEFORE CHRISTMAS

# The Night Before Christmas

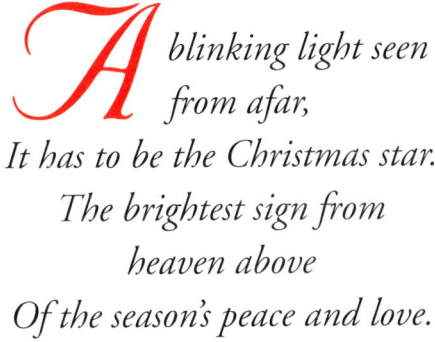

*A blinking light seen from afar,
It has to be the Christmas star.
The brightest sign from heaven above
Of the season's peace and love.*

## THE NIGHT BEFORE CHRISTMAS

*Christmas trees in
all shapes and sizes
Soon will be filled with
sweet surprises.
Trimmed in tradition and
glowing with cheer,
Greeting the holiday and
the New Year.*

# The Night Before Christmas

# THE NIGHT BEFORE CHRISTMAS

## The Night Before Christmas

*Happiness is walking through the new fallen snow and looking back to see your footsteps following you and looking ahead to the unmarked winter wonderland.*

# THE NIGHT BEFORE CHRISTMAS

# The Night Before Christmas

*C herish the magical season*
*H olly wrapped around*
*the staircase*
*R ed ribbons adorning gifts*
*great and small*
*I cicles dripping from rooftops*
*S nowmen greeting passersby*
*T eddie bears under the tree*
*M arshmallows roasting in the fireplace*
*A ngels perched atop the Christmas tree*
*S hoppers bustling in the crowds.*

# THE NIGHT BEFORE CHRISTMAS

*As you hang each ornament on the tree, remember a friend, remember a family member, remember a wonderful moment—and make each ornament a memory to cherish.*